Let's Swim

by Rebecca Fox

 HOUGHTON MIFFLIN   BOSTON

PHOTOGRAPHY CREDITS: Cover © Mira; Toc © Jeff Rotman/Alamy; 2 © Masterfile (Royalty-Free Div.); 3 © Brock May/ Photo Researchers, Inc.; 4 © Jeff Rotman/Alamy; 5 © Hiroya Minakuchi/Minden Pictures; 6 © Mira

Printed in China

ISBN-13: 978-0-547-01848-5
ISBN-10: 0-547-01848-7

8 9 10 0940 16 15 14 13
4500408731

The fish can swim.

The ducks can swim.

The seals can swim.

The whales can swim.

I can swim!

Responding

Author's Purpose

Tell why the author wrote this book. List three things that can swim. Make a chart.

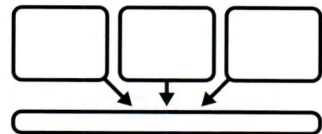

✏ **Write About It**

Text to World Draw a picture of things swimming in the sea. Label the things in your picture. Tell about your picture.

WORDS TO KNOW

be	will

✔ **TARGET SKILL** **Author's Purpose**
Tell why an author writes a book.

✔ **TARGET STRATEGY** **Analyze/Evaluate**
Tell how you feel about the text, and why.

GENRE **Informational text** gives facts about a topic.